MW01206630

V-Stitches & Ruffles

EASY

Sizes

Instructions given fit woman's small; changes for medium, large, X-large and 2X-large are in [ ].

Finished Garment Measurements

Hips: Approximatley 36 inches *(small)* [40 inches *(medium)*, 44 inches *(large)*, 48 inches *(X-large)*, 52 inches *(2X-large)*]

Materials

- Patons Brilliant light (DK) weight yarn (1¾ oz/166 yds/50g per ball): 17 [18, 19, 20, 21] balls #04430 beautiful burgundy
- Size H/8/5mm crochet hook or size needed to obtain gauge
- Tapestry needle
- 1-inch-wide elastic: waist measurement less 1 inch
- Large safety pin
- Sewing needle and matching thread

3 LIGHT

Gauge

7 dc and 2 rows = 2 inches

Special Stitch

V-stitch (V-st):
In st indicated work (dc, ch 1, dc).

Pattern Note

Skirt is worked from waist to hem.

Instructions

Row 1 (RS): Ch 136 [142, 157, 172, 187]; dc in 4th ch from hook *(beg 3 sk chs count as a dc)* and in each rem ch, turn. *(134 [140, 155, 170, 185] dc)*

Row 2: Ch 3 *(counts as a dc on this and following rows)*, dc in each dc and in 3rd ch of beg 3 sk chs, turn.

Row 3: Ch 3, dc in each dc and in 3rd ch of turning ch-3, turn.

Rows 4 & 5: Rep row 3.

Note: Rows 1–5 form casing for waistband elastic.

Row 6: Ch 3, sk next dc; *in next dc work V-st *(see Special Stitch)*; sk next 2 dc; rep from * to last 2 dc and turning ch-3; in next dc work V-st; sk last dc, dc in 3rd ch of turning ch-3, turn. *(44 [46, 51, 56, 61] V-sts)*

Row 7: Ch 3, V-st in ch-1 sp of each V-st; dc in 3rd ch of turning ch-3, turn.

Row 8–21: Rep row 7.

Row 22: Ch 3, 4 dc in ch-1 sp of each V-st; dc in 3rd ch of turning ch-3, turn. *(178 [186, 206, 226, 246] dc)*

Row 23: Ch 3, working in **front lps** *(see Stitch Guide)* only, 3 dc in each dc; dc in 3rd ch of turning ch-3. Fasten off.

Row 24: Hold piece with WS facing you; join in same ch as last dc of previous row made; ch 3, working in unused lps of row 22, sk next 1 [1, 0, 1,1] lp; *V-st in next lp; sk next 2 lps; rep from * to last 4 [3, 4, 4, 3] lps and turning ch-3; V-st in next lp; sk next 3 [2, 2, 3, 2] lps, dc in 3rd ch of turning ch-3, turn. *(58 [61, 68, 74, 81] V-sts)*

Rows 25–39: Rep row 7.

Row 40: Ch 3, 4 dc in ch-1 sp of each V-st; dc in 3rd ch of turning ch-3, turn. *(234 [246, 274, 298, 326] dc)*

Row 41: Rep row 23.

Row 42: Hold piece with WS facing you; working behind dc make on previous row, join in same ch as last dc of previous row made; ch 3, working in unused lps of row 40, sk next 1 [1, 1, 1, 0] lp; *V-st in next lp; sk next 2 lps; rep from * to last 3 [3, 3, 4, 1] lp(s) and turning ch-3; V-st in next lp; sk next 2 [2, 3, 3, 0] lps, dc in 3rd ch of turning ch-3, turn. *(77 [81, 90, 98, 108] V-sts)*

Row 43–55: Rep row 7.

For Sizes Small & Medium Only

Row 56: Ch 3; *4 dc in ch-1 sp of each V-st, 3 dc in ch-1 sp of next V-st; rep from * to last V-st; 3 dc in ch-1 sp of last V-st; dc in 3rd ch of turning ch-3, turn. *(271 [285] dc)*
Continue with For All Sizes.

For Sizes Large, X-Large & 2X-Large Only

Row 56: Ch 3; *4 dc in ch-1 sp of each V-st, 3 dc in ch-1 sp of next V-st; rep from * to turning ch-3; dc in 3rd ch of turning ch-3, turn. *(317 [345, 380] dc)*
Continue with For All Sizes.

For All Sizes

Row 57: Rep row 22.

Row 58: Hold piece with WS facing you; working behind dc make on previous row, join in same ch as last dc of previous row made; ch 3, working in unused lps of row 56, sk next 1 [1, 0, 1, 0] dc; *V-st in next dc; sk next 2 dc; rep from * to last 2 [1, 1, 2, 0] dc and turning ch-3; V-st in next dc sk next 1 [0, 0, 1, 0] dc, dc in 3rd ch of turning ch-3, turn. *(89 [94, 105, 114, 126] V-sts)*

Row 59–71: Rep row 7.

Row 72: Rep row 22.

Row 73: Ch 3, 3 dc in each dc; dc in 3rd ch of turning ch-3.

Fasten off and weave in all ends.

Finishing

Sew edges tog, forming back seam. Fold casing to inside and whipstitch in place, leaving 3–4 inches unsewn. Pin safety pin to 1 end of elastic and draw elastic through casing. With sewing needle and matching thread and overlapping ends ½ inch, sew ends tog securely. Sew opening closed.

Ruffled Stockinette

EASY

Sizes

Woman's small (medium, large, extra-large, 2X-large) Instructions are given for smallest size, with larger sizes in parentheses. When only 1 number is given, it applies to all sizes.

Finished Garment Measurements

Hips: Approx 36 (40, 44, 48, 52) inches

Materials

- TLC Cotton Plus medium weight yarn (186 yds/3.5 oz/100g per skein): 5 (5, 6, 7, 8) skeins tangerine #3252
- Size 10 (6mm) 29-inch circular knitting needle or size needed to obtain gauge
- Tapestry needle
- ¾-inch-wide elastic measuring one inch less than waist

4 MEDIUM

Gauge

16 sts and 20 rows = 4 inches/10cm in St st
To save time, take time to check gauge.

Pattern Notes

Skirt is worked from hem to waist.
Circular needle is used to accommodate large number of sts. Do not join; work back and forth in rows.

Instructions

Front/Back

Make 2

Bell Border

Using cable cast on (page 13), cast on 219 (243, 267, 291, 315) sts.

Row 1 (RS): P3, *k9, p3; rep from * to end.

Row 2: K3, *p9, k3; rep from * to end.

Row 3: P3, *wyib, sl 1, k1, psso, k5, k2tog, p3; rep from * to end. (183, 203, 223, 243, 263 sts)

Row 4: K3, *p7, k3; rep from * to end.

Row 5: P3, *wyib, sl 1, k1, psso, k3, k2tog, p3; rep from * to end. (147, 163, 179, 195, 211 sts)

Row 6: K3, *p5, k3; rep from * to end.

Row 7: P3, *wyib, sl 1, k1, psso, k1, k2tog, p3; rep from * to end. (111, 123, 135, 147, 159 sts)

Row 8: K3, *p3, k3; rep from * to end.

Row 9: P3, *wyib, sl 1, k2tog, psso, p3; rep from * to end. (75, 83, 91, 99, 107 sts)

Row 10: K3, *p1, k3; rep from * to end.

Row 11: P3, *k1, p3; rep from * to end.

Row 12: K3, *p1, k3; rep from * to end.

Upper Skirt

Row 13: Knit to last 2 sts, dec. (74, 82, 90, 98, 106 sts)

Row 14: Purl across.

Row 15: Knit across.

Rep Rows 14 and 15 until skirt measures approx 26 inches ending with a WS row.

Waistband Casing

Row 1 (RS): Purl.

Row 2: Purl.

Row 3: Knit.

Rows 4–13: [Rep rows 2 and 3] 5 times.

Row 14: Rep row 2.

Bind off all sts.

Assembly

Sew side seams. Fold casing to inside and sew in place, leaving 2 inches open for elastic. Insert elastic. Sew ends of elastic together to secure. Sew last 2 inches closed.

EASY

Sizes

Instructions given fit woman's small; changes for medium, large, X-large and 2X-large are in [ ].

Finished Garment Measurements

Hips: approximately 36 inches *(small)* [40 inches *(medium)*, 44 inches *(large)*, 48½ inches *(X-large)*, 52½ inches *(2X-large)*]

Materials

- TLC Cotton Plus medium (worsted) weight yarn (3½ oz/186 yds/100g per ball): 8 [9, 10, 11, 12] balls #3642 kiwi
- Size H/8/5mm crochet hook or size needed to obtain gauge
- Tapestry needle
- 1-inch-wide elastic: waist measurement less 1 inch
- Large safety pin
- Sewing needle and matching thread

4 MEDIUM

Gauge

3 shells = 4½ inches

Special Stitch

V-stitch (V-st):

In st indicated work (dc, ch 1, dc).

Pattern Note

Skirt is worked from waist to hem.

Instructions

Row 1: Ch 134 [149, 164, 179, 194]; dc in 4th ch from hook *(beg 3 sk chs count as a dc)* and in each rem ch, turn. *(132 [147, 162, 177, 192] dc)*

Row 2: Ch 3 *(counts as a dc on this and following rows)*, dc in each dc and in 3rd ch of beg 3 sk chs, turn.

Row 3: Ch 3, dc in each dc and in 3rd ch of turning ch-3, turn.

Row 4: Rep row 3.

Row 5: Ch 3, sk next 2 dc; *in next dc work (2 dc, ch 1, 2 dc)—*shell made*; sk next 4 dc; rep from * to last 3 dc and turning ch-3; in next dc work (2 dc, ch 1, 2 dc)—*shell made*; sk last 2 dc, dc in 3rd ch of turning ch-3; turn.

Row 6: Ch 3, shell in ch-1 sp of each shell; dc in 3rd ch of turning ch-3.

Rows 7–16: Rep row 6.

Row 17: Ch 3, in ch-1 sp of each shell work (3 dc, ch 1, 3 dc)—*large shell made*; dc in 3rd ch of turning ch-3, turn.

Row 18: Ch 3, in ch-1 sp of each large shell work large shell; dc in 3rd ch of turning ch-3, turn.

Rows 19–35: Rep row 11.

Row 36: Ch 3, 4 dc in first dc; *large shell in ch-1 sp of each of next 2 large shells; 9 dc in ch-1 sp of next shell; rep from * to last 2 large shells; large shell in ch-1 sp of each of last 2 shells; 5 dc in 3rd ch of turning ch-3, turn.

Row 37: Ch 4 *(counts as a dc and a ch-1 sp)*, [dc in next dc, ch 1] 4 times; *large shell in each of next 2 large shells; ch 1, sk next 3 dc of last large shell, [dc in next dc, ch 1] 9 times; rep from * to last 2 large shells; large shell in last 2 shells; ch 1, sk next 3 dc of last large shell, [dc in next dc, ch 1] 4 times; dc in 3rd ch of turning ch-3, turn.

Row 38: Ch 3, [sc in next ch-1 sp, ch 3] 4 times; *3 dc in ch-1 sp of next shell; ch 1, 3 dc in ch-1 sp of next shell; ch 3, sk next ch-1 sp, [sc in next ch-1 sp, ch 3] 8 times; rep from * to last 2 shells; 3 dc in ch-1 sp of next shell; ch 1, 3 dc in ch-1 sp of last shell; ch 3, sk next ch-1 sp, [sc in next ch-1 sp, ch 3] 3 times; sc in sp formed by turning ch-4, turn.

Row 39: Ch 1, sc in first sc, ch 3, [sc in next ch-1 sp, ch 3] 3 times; *large shell in next ch-1 sp; ch 3, [sc in next ch-1 sp, ch 3] 7 times; rep from * to last ch-1 sp between 3-dc groups; large shell in last ch-1 sp; ch 3, [sc in next ch-1 sp, ch 3] 3 times; sc in sp formed by turning ch-3, turn.

Row 40: Ch 3, [sc in next ch-3 sp, ch 3] 3 times; *large shell in next large shell; ch 3, [sc in next ch-3 sp, ch 3] 6 times; rep from * to last large shell; large shell in last large shell; ch 3, [sc in next ch-3 sp, ch 3] twice, sc in next ch-3 sp, ch 1, dc in last sc, turn.

Row 41: Ch 1, sc in next ch-1 sp, [ch 3, sc in next ch-3 sp] twice; ch 3; * in ch-1 sp of next large shell work (2 dc, ch 1, 2 dc, ch 1, 2 dc); ch 3, [sc in next ch-3 sp, ch 3] 5 times; rep from * to last large shell; ch 3, in ch-1 sp of last large shell work (2 dc, ch 1, 2 dc, ch 1, 2 dc); ch 3, [sc in next ch-3 sp, ch 3] twice; sc in sp formed by turning ch-3, turn.

Row 42: Ch 3, [sc in next ch-3 sp, ch 3] twice; *shell in next ch-1 sp, ch 1, shell in next ch-1 sp; ch 3, [sc in next ch-3 sp, ch 3] 4 times; rep from * to last 2 ch-1 sps; shell in next ch-1 sp; ch 1, shell in last ch-1 sp; ch 3, sc in next ch-3 sp, ch 3, sc in next ch-3 sp, ch 1, dc in turning ch-1, turn.

Row 43: Ch 1, sc in first dc, ch 3, sc in next ch-3 sp; ch 3; *shell in each of next 3 ch-1 sps; ch 3, [sc in next ch-3 sp, ch 3] 3 times; rep from * to last 3 ch-1 sps; shell in each of last 3 ch-1 sps; ch 3, [sc in next ch-3 sp, ch 3, sc in sp formed by turning ch-3, turn.

Row 44: Ch 3, sc in next ch-3 sp; ch 3; *[shell in ch-1 sp of next shell, ch 2] twice; shell in ch-1 sp of next shell; ch 3, [sc in next ch-3 sp, ch 3] twice; rep from * to last 3 shells; [shell in ch-1 sp of next shell, ch 2] twice; shell in ch-1 sp of last shell; ch 3, sc in next ch-3 sp, ch 1, sc in turning ch-1, turn.

Row 45: Ch 1, sc in first dc, ch 3, *shell in next shell; ch 2, 9 dc in ch-1 sp of next shell; ch 2, shell in ch-1 sp of next shell; ch 3, sc in next ch-3 sp, ch 3; rep from * to last 3 shells; shell in next shell, ch 2, 9 dc in ch-1 sp of next shell, ch 2, shell in last shell; ch 3, sc in sp formed by turning ch-3.

Fasten off and weave in ends.

Finishing

Sew edges tog forming back seam. Fold casing to inside and whipstitch in place, leaving 3–4 inches unsewn. Pin safety pin to 1 end of elastic and draw elastic through casing. With sewing needle and matching thread and overlapping ends ½ inch, sew ends tog securely. Sew opening closed.

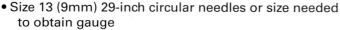

Tiered Drop-Stitch

EASY

Sizes

Woman's small (medium, large, extra-large, 2X-large)

Finished Garment Measurements

Hips: Approximately 36 (40, 44, 48, 52) inches

Materials

• Moda Dea Spellbound bulky weight yarn (93 yds/50g per ball): 6 (7, 8, 9, 10) balls merlin #2753
• Size 13 (9mm) 29-inch circular needles or size needed to obtain gauge
• Yarn needle
• 1-inch-wide elastic measuring 1 inch less than waist

Gauge

14 sts and 16 rows = 4 inches/10 cm in garter st
To save time, take time to check gauge.

Pattern Notes

Skirt is worked from waist to hem with seam at back. Circular needle is used to accommodate large number of sts. Do not join; work back and forth in rows.

Instructions

Cast on 128 (142, 154, 168, 182) sts.

Waist casing

Row 1 (RS): Knit.
Row 2: Purl.
Rows 3–8: [Rep rows 1 and 2] 3 times.

Body

Work in garter st until piece measures 8 inches from beg of garter st, ending with WS row.

Tier 1 Drop Stitch

Row 1 (RS): *K1, wrapping yarn twice around needle; rep from * across.

Row 2: Knit across, dropping extra wrap from needle.

[Rep Rows 1 and 2] twice.

Tier 2 Drop Stitch

Row 1: *K1, wrapping yarn 3 times around needle; rep from * across.

Row 2: Knit across, dropping extra 2 wraps from needle.

[Rep Rows 1 and 2] twice.

Tier 3 Drop Stitch

Row 1: *K1, wrapping yarn 4 times around needle; rep from * across.

Row 2: Knit across, dropping extra 3 wraps from needle.

Rep Rows 1 and 2 until skirt measures approx 28 inches from beg of garter st.

Bind off as loosely as possible.

Assembly

Sew back seam, leaving ribbon free for each drop-stitch row, then securing on next row.

Fold casing to inside and sew in place leaving 3 inches open for elastic. Insert elastic and sew ends of elastic tog to secure. Sew opening closed.

EASY

Sizes

Instructions given fit woman's small; changes for medium, large, X-large and 2X-large are in [ ].

Finished Garment Measurements

Hips: Approximately 36 inches *(small)* [40 inches *(medium)*, 44 inches *(large)*, 48 inches *(X-large)*, 52 inches *(2X-large)*]

Materials

• Aunt Lydia's Fashion Crochet size 3 crochet cotton (150 yds per ball):
  8 [9, 10, 12, 12] balls #377 tan
• Sizes F/5/3.75mm, H/8/5mm and I/9/5.5mm crochet hooks or sizes needed to obtain gauge
• Tapestry needle
• 1-inch-wide elastic: waist measurement less 1 inch
• Large safety pin
• Sewing needle and matching thread

Gauge

F hook: 3 shells = 4 inches
H hook: 2 shells = 3 inches
I hook: 3 shells = 5 inches

Special Stitch

V-stitch (V-st):

In st indicated work (dc, ch 1, dc).

Pattern Note

Skirt is worked from waist to hem.

Instructions

Row 1: With F hook, ch 147 [165, 183, 195, 213]; dc in 4th ch from hook *(beg 3 sk chs count as a dc)* and in each rem ch, turn. *(145 [163, 181, 193, 211] dc)*

Row 2: Ch 3 *(counts as a dc on this and following rows)*, dc in each dc and in 3rd ch of beg 3 sk chs, turn.

Row 3: Ch 3, dc in each dc and in 3rd ch of turning ch-3, turn.

Rows 4 & 5: Rep row 3.

Note: Rows 1–5 form casing for waistband elastic.

Row 6: Ch 3, 2 dc in first dc; *sk next 2 dc, sc in dc, sk next 2 dc, 5 dc in next dc—*shell made*; rep from * to last 2 dc and turning ch-3; sk last 2 dc, sc in 3rd ch of turning ch-3, turn. *(24 [27, 30, 32, 35] shells)*

Row 7: Ch 3, 2 dc in first sc; *sk next 2 dc, sc in next dc, sk next 2 dc, shell in next sc; rep from * to last 2 dc and turning ch-3; sk last 2 dc, sc in 3rd ch of turning ch-3, turn.

Row 8: Ch 3, 2 dc in first sc; *sk next 2 dc, sc in dc, sk next 2 dc, shell in next sc; rep from * to last 2 dc and turning ch-3; sk last 2 dc, sc in 3rd ch of turning ch-3, turn.

Row 9: Ch 3, 2 dc in first sc; *sk next 2 dc, sc in next dc, sk next 2 dc, shell in next sc; rep from * to last 2 dc and turning ch-3; sk last 2 dc, sc in 3rd ch of turning ch-3, turn.

Rep rows 8 and 9 until length from row 6 measures approximately 8 inches.

Change to H hook and rep rows 8 and 9 until length from row 6 measures approximately 16½ inches.

Change to I hook and rep rows 8 and 9 until length from row 6 measures approximately 25 inches.

Shell Border

For Size Small Only

Foundation row: Ch 1, [sc in next 23 sts, 2 sc in next st] 6 times; sc in 3rd ch of turning ch-3. *(151 sc)*

Continue with For All Sizes.

For Size Medium Only

Foundation row: Ch 1, 2 sc in first st; sc in next 80 sts, 2 sc in next st; sc in next 80 sts, 2 sc in 3rd ch of turning ch-3. *(166 sc)*

Continue with For All Sizes.

For Sizes Large & 2X-Large Only

Foundation row: Ch 1; sc in each st and in 3rd ch of turning ch-3, turn. *(181 [211] sc)*

Continue with For All Sizes.

For Size X-Large Only

Foundation row: Ch 1, 2 sc in first st; sc in next 95 sts, 2 sc in next st; sc in next 95 sts, 2 sc in 3rd ch of turning ch-3. *(196 sc)*

Continue with For All Sizes.

For All Sizes

Row 1: Ch 3 *(counts as a dc and a ch-1 sp)*, sk next sc; *in next sc work **V-st** *(see Special Stitch)*; sk next 2 sc; rep from * to last 3 sc; in next sc work V-st, sk next sc, dc in last sc, turn. *(50 [55, 60, 65, 70] V-sts)*

Row 2: Ch 5 *(counts as a dc and a ch-2 sp)*; *sc in ch-1 sp of next V-st, ch 5; rep from * to last V-st; sc in ch-1 sp of last V-st, ch 2, dc in 3rd ch of turning ch-3, turn.

Row 3: Ch 3 *(counts as a dc)*, 4 dc in next ch-2 sp; *[sc in next ch-5 sp, ch 5] 3 times; sc in next ch-5 sp, 7 dc in next ch-5 sp—*shell made;* rep from * to last 4 ch-5 sps; [sc in next ch-5 sp, ch 5] 3 times; sc in last ch-5 sp, 5 dc in sp formed by turning ch-5, turn.

Row 4: Ch 4 *(counts as a dc and a ch-1 sp)*; [dc in next dc, ch 1] 3 times; dc in next dc; *[sc in next ch-5 sp, ch 5] twice; sc in next ch-5 sp, [dc in next dc, ch 1] 6 times; dc in next dc; rep from * to last 3 ch-5 sps; [sc in next ch-5 sp, ch 5] twice; sc in next ch-5 sp, [dc in next dc, ch 1] 4 times; dc in 3rd ch of turning ch-3, turn.

Row 5: Ch 5 *(counts as a dc and a ch-2 sp)*, [dc in next dc, ch 2] 3 times; dc in next dc; *sc in next ch-5 sp, ch 5, sc in next ch-5 sp, [dc in next dc, ch 2] 6 times; dc in next dc; rep from * to last 2 ch-5 sps; sc in next ch-5 sp, ch 5, sc in next ch-5 sp, [dc in next dc, ch 2] 4 times; dc in 3rd ch of turning ch-4, turn.

Row 6: Ch 6, sl st in 3rd ch from hook—*picot made*; [dc in next dc, ch 3, sl st in 3rd ch from hook—*picot made*] 4 times; *sc in next ch-5 sp, picot; [dc in next dc, picot] 7 times; rep from * to last ch-5 sp; sc in last ch-5 sp, picot; [dc in next dc, picot] 4 times; dc in 3rd ch of turning ch-5.

Fasten off and weave in all ends.

Finishing

Sew edges tog, forming back seam. Fold casing to inside and whipstitch in place, leaving 3–4 inches unsewn. Pin safety pin to 1 end of elastic and draw elastic through casing. With sewing needle and matching thread and overlapping ends ½ inch, sew ends tog securely. Sew opening closed.

Crochet Abbreviations & Symbols

beg	beg/beginning
bpdc	back post double crochet
bphdc	back post half double crochet
bpsc	back post single crochet
bptr	back post treble crochet
CC	contrasting color
ch	chain stitch
ch-	refers to chain or space previously made (i.e., ch-1 space)
ch sp	chain space
cl(s)	cluster(s)
cm	centimeters(s)
dc	double crochet
dec	decrease/decreases/decreasing
dtr	double treble crochet
fpdc	front post double crochet
fphdc	front post half double crochet
fpsc	front post single crochet
fptr	front post treble crochet
g	gram(s)
hdc	half double crochet
inc	increase/increases/increasing
lp(s)	loop(s)
MC	main color
mm	millimeter(s)
oz	ounce(s)
pc	popcorn
rem	rem/remaining
rep	repeat(s)
rnd(s)	round(s)
RS	right side
sc	single crochet
sk	skip
sl st	slip stitch
sp(s)	space(s)
st(s)	stitch(es)
tog	together
tr	treble crochet
trtr	triple treble crochet
WS	wrong side
yd(s)	yard(s)
yo	yarn over

* An asterisk is used to mark the beginning of a portion of instructions to be worked more than once; thus, "rep from * twice more" means after working the instructions once, repeat the instructions following the asterisk twice more (3 times in all).

[ ] Brackets are used to enclose instructions that are to be worked the number of times indicated after the brackets. For example, "[2 dc in next st, sk next st] 5 times" means to follow the instructions within the brackets a total of 5 times.

( ) Parentheses are used to enclose a group of stitches that are worked in one space or stitch. For example, "(2 dc, ch 2, 2 dc) in next st" means to work all the stitches within the parentheses in the next space or stitch. Parentheses are also used to enclose special instructions or stitch counts.

Knit Abbreviations & Symbols

approx ....approximately
beg.. begin/beginning
CC .... contrasting color
ch.. chain stitch
cm ....centimeter(s)
cn ....cable needle
dec .... decrease/decreases/decreasing
dpn(s) .... double-pointed needle(s)
g ....gram
inc ....increase/increases/increasing
k...knit
k2tog...................................... knit 2 stitches together
LH...left hand
lp(s)..loop(s)
m.. meter(s)
M1 .... make one stitch
MC .... main color
mm ....millimeter(s)
oz...ounce(s)
p ....purl
pat(s)..pattern(s)
p2tog .... purl 2 stitches together
psso .... pass slipped stitch over
p2sso .... pass 2 slipped stitches over
rem .... remain/remaining
rep..repeat(s)
rev St st .... reverse stockinette stitch
RH ....right hand

rnd(s) ....rounds
RS ....right side
skp ....slip, knit, pass stitch over—one stitch decreased
sk2p .... slip 1, knit 2 together, pass slip stitch
....................over the knit 2 together; 2 stitches have been decreased
sl..slip
sl 1k .... slip 1 knitwise
sl 1p ....slip 1 purlwise
sl st.. slip stitch(es)
ssk.....................slip, slip, knit these 2 stitches together—a decrease
st(s) .... stitch(es)
St st..................................... stockinette stitch/stocking stitch
tbl...through back loop(s)
tog... together
WS .... wrong side
wyib .... with yarn in back
wyif ....with yarn in front
yd(s)...yard(s)
yfwd.. yarn forward
yo .... yarn over

[ ] work instructions within brackets as many times as directed

( ) work instructions within parentheses in the place directed

** repeat instructions following the asterisks as directed

* repeat instructions following the single asterisk as directed

" inch(es)

Cable Cast On

This type of cast on is used for a firmer edge.
Make a slip knot on the left needle.

Insert the right needle between the last two stitches on the left needle. Knit a stitch and place it on the left needle. Repeat for each stitch needed.

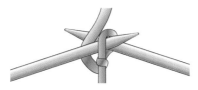

Fig. 1

Knit a stitch in this knot and place it on the left needle.

Fig. 3

Fig. 2

Standard Yarn Weight System

Categories of yarn, gauge ranges, and recommended needle and hook sizes

Yarn Weight Symbol & Category Names	1 SUPER FINE	2 FINE	3 LIGHT	4 MEDIUM	5 BULKY	6 SUPER BULKY
Type of Yarns in Category	Sock, Fingering, Baby	Sport, Baby	DK, Light Worsted	Worsted, Afghan, Aran	Chunky, Craft, Rug	Bulky, Roving
Crochet Gauge* Ranges in Single Crochet to 4 inch	21–32 sts	16–20 sts	12–17 sts	11–14 sts	8–11 sts	5–9 sts
Recommended Hook in Metric Size Range	2.25–3.5mm	3.5–4.5mm	4.5–5.5mm	5.5–6.5mm	6.5–9mm	9mm and larger
Recommended Hook U.S. Size Range	B/1–E/4	E/4–7	7–I/9	I/9–K/10½	K/10½–M/13	M/13 and larger
Knit Gauge Range* in Stockinette Stitch to 4 inches	27–32 sts	23–26 sts	21–24 sts	16–20 sts	12–15 sts	6–11 sts
Recommended Needle in Metric Size Range	2.25–3.25mm	3.25–3.75mm	3.75–4.5mm	4.5–5.5mm	5.5–8mm	8mm and larger
Recommended Needle U.S. Size Range	1 to 3	3 to 5	5 to 7	7 to 9	9 to 11	11 and larger

* GUIDELINES ONLY: The above reflect the most commonly used gauges and hook or needle sizes for specific yarn categories.

Skill Levels

BEGINNER
Beginner projects using basic stitches. Minimal shaping.

EASY
Easy projects using basic stitches, repetitive stitch patterns, simple color changes and simple shaping and finishing.

INTERMEDIATE
Intermediate projects with a variety of stitches, mid-level shaping and finishing.

EXPERIENCED
Experienced projects using advanced techniques and stitches, detailed shaping and refined finishing.

Stitch Guide

CROCHET HOOKS

Metric	US	Metric	US
.60mm	14	3.00mm	D/3
.75mm	12	3.50mm	E/4
1.00mm	10	4.00mm	F/5
1.50mm	6	4.50mm	G/6
1.75mm	5	5.00mm	H/8
2.00mm	B/1	5.50mm	I/9
2.50mm	C/2	6.00mm	J/10

Chain—ch: Yo, pull through lp on hook.

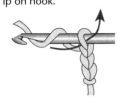

Slip stitch—sl st: Insert hook in st, yo, pull through both lps on hook.

Front loop—front lp
Back loop—back lp

Front Loop   Back Loop

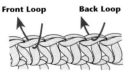

Single crochet—sc: Insert hook in st, yo, pull through st, yo, pull through both lps on hook.

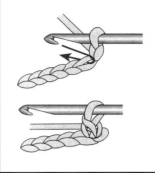

Reverse single crochet—reverse sc: Working from left to right, insert hook in next st, complete as sc.

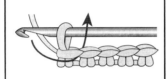

Front post stitch—fp: Back post stitch—bp: When working post st, insert hook from right to left around post st on previous row.

Back   Front

Post of Stitch

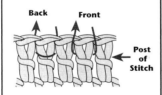

Half double crochet—hdc: Yo, insert hook in st, yo, pull through st, yo, pull through all 3 lps on hook.

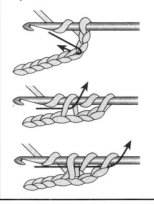

Double crochet—dc: Yo, insert hook in st, yo, pull through st, [yo, pull through 2 lps] twice.

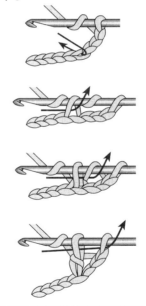

Change colors: Drop first color; with second color, pull through last 2 lps of st.

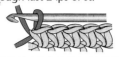

Treble crochet—tr: Yo twice, insert hook in st, yo, pull through st, [yo, pull through 2 lps] 3 times.

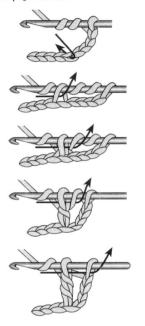

Double treble crochet—dtr: Yo 3 times, insert hook in st, yo, pull through st, [yo, pull through 2 lps] 4 times.

Single crochet decrease (sc dec): (Insert hook, yo, draw up a lp) in each of the sts indicated, yo, draw through all lps on hook.

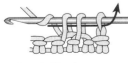

Example of 2-sc dec

Half double crochet decrease (hdc dec): (Yo, insert hook, yo, draw lp through) in each of the sts indicated, yo, draw through all lps on hook.

Double crochet decrease (dc dec): (Yo, insert hook, yo, draw lp through, yo, draw through 2 lps on hook) in each of the sts indicated, yo, draw through all lps on hook.

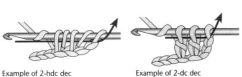

Example of 2-hdc dec   Example of 2-dc dec

US		UK
sl st (slip stitch)	=	sc (single crochet)
sc (single crochet)	=	dc (double crochet)
hdc (half double crochet)	=	htr (half treble crochet)
dc (double crochet)	=	tr (treble crochet)
tr (treble crochet)	=	dtr (double treble crochet)
dtr (double treble crochet)	=	ttr (triple treble crochet)
skip	=	miss

For more complete information, visit

StitchGuide.com

Metric Charts

INCHES INTO MILLIMETERS & CENTIMETERS (Rounded off slightly)

inches	mm	cm	inches	cm	inches	cm	inches	cm
1/8	3	0.3	5	12.5	21	53.5	38	96.5
1/4	6	0.6	5 1/2	14	22	56	39	99
3/8	10	1	6	15	23	58.5	40	101.5
1/2	13	1.3	7	18	24	61	41	104
5/8	15	1.5	8	20.5	25	63.5	42	106.5
3/4	20	2	9	23	26	66	43	109
7/8	22	2.2	10	25.5	27	68.5	44	112
1	25	2.5	11	28	28	71	45	114.5
1 1/4	32	3.2	12	30.5	29	73.5	46	117
1 1/2	38	3.8	13	33	30	76	47	119.5
1 3/4	45	4.5	14	35.5	31	79	48	122
2	50	5	15	38	32	81.5	49	124.5
2 1/2	65	6.5	16	40.5	33	84	50	127
3	75	7.5	17	43	34	86.5		
3 1/2	90	9	18	46	35	89		
4	100	10	19	48.5	36	91.5		
4 1/2	115	11.5	20	51	37	94		

KNITTING NEEDLE CONVERSION CHART

U.S.	1	2	3	4	5	6	7	8	9	10	10½	11	13	15	17	19	35	50
Continental-mm	2.25	2.75	3.25	3.5	3.75	4	4.5	5	5.5	6	6.5	8	9	10	12.75	15	19	25

CROCHET HOOKS CONVERSION CHART

U.S.	B/1	C/2	D/3	E/4	F/5	G/6	H/8	I/9	J/10	K/10½	N
Continental-mm	2.25	2.75	3.25	3.5	3.75	4	5	5.5	6	6.5	9

American School of Needlework®
excellence in instruction

DRG Publishing
306 East Parr Road
Berne, IN 46711
©2006 American School of Needlework

TOLL-FREE ORDER LINE or to request a free catalog (800) 582-6643
Customer Service (800) 282-6643, **Fax** (800) 882-6643

Visit AnniesAttic.com.

We have made every effort to ensure the accuracy and completeness of these instructions.
We cannot, however, be responsible for human error, typographical mistakes or variations in individual work.

ISBN: 978-1-59012-178-8   All rights reserved.   Printed in USA   2 3 4 5 6 7 8 9